T0090687

FAITH & FIGHT

AN INUPIAT STRUGGLE WITH GOOD & EVIL

CRYSTAL F FERGUSON QIĠÑAK BREITHAUPT

WESTBOW
PRESS®
A DIVISION OF THOMAS NELSON
& ZONDERVAN

WestBow Press books may be ordered through booksellers or by contacting:

WestBow Press
A Division of Thomas Nelson & Zondervan
1663 Liberty Drive
Bloomington, IN 47403
www.westbowpress.com
844-714-3454

ISBN: 979-8-3850-0868-1 (sc)
ISBN: 979-8-3850-0869-8 (e)

Library of Congress Control Number: 2023918848

Print information available on the last page.

WestBow Press rev. date: 10/19/2023

DEDICATION

I would first like to dedicate this to my Lord and Savior who knew me when I was being created in my mother's womb. To David for always being patient, loving, supportive and putting up with a daddy's girl. To my children who are my everything. I could never be prouder of anything in my life than being called, 'Mom' by you three and now your beautiful and talented spouses, then making me an Ahna to the most precious babes ever. To the friends I made in Arizona, and in Forks, WA too, especially my third mom, Bernice. To my Bethie, I love you forever! To my Bud, Tia, I would have never done any of this if it were not first for your strength. To Paulette, I love you. To my sis, Cheree, I think everyone will know how I feel about you.

STRENGTH

For the past nine years, since I lost my mother, I have been dealing with my pain simply by harming myself and my family. You see, at mom's funeral one of my cousins was in line to hug and comfort my family for the loss of my mother. I didn't see it coming, it just happened. In that instant I am standing in front of the church being held and comforted by someone I wish I wasn't. In that moment, I cannot tell you how dirty I felt. I thought the whole room could feel and see this disgusting and vile exchange. I couldn't push him away, what would everyone think? But I also couldn't believe it was happening. I felt the abuse all over again only this time there was an audience, in the church, no less!

My auntie just passed away, I am so very thankful that I was able to be there and hug and love my family. It was such a struggle to even have the courage to be present. But since I have started this process, I've gained a strength I never knew I possessed. At times, I have so much courage, ego, pride, determination and belief in myself that it drives everyone around me wild. On this one, I felt like a coward. However, I did not know when I would see the rest of my family again, because I live in Oregon. I knew I had to go to my aunt's funeral. So, I did. I mustered up the strength to go. I decided none of them know what I have been dealing with. I am not going to be a victim, but I don't see myself as a survivor either.

I think it's like the first tattoo I got. It represents faith, hope and love and that is exactly why I got it. That is how I see myself; I have always leaned hard on those three things, and I think they accurately depict my life and me. I have faith in the Lord to do better things in my life and through me. I have always had hope in people to do and be better. And hope for my future. And whether a friend or a family member, I had love to give and love to offer. But it took everything in me to hold out my arm and tell one of my relatives, "I have nothing for you!" I cannot tell you I am whole, and I cannot tell you I am healed, but with an incredible support system and the Lord, I will keep going and the future looks amazing. I want my family, my sisters, my nieces, my granddaughter, my future great granddaughters to know their worth! Drinking only leads to destruction for generations. Break the cycle. Be who your parents couldn't quite be. Be better.

DO YOU KNOW THE TIME?

My dad had just taken me to visit the University of Alaska Southeast in Juneau (UAS). This was the school I was certain I wanted to go to. None of my siblings chose this school but I knew it was where I wanted to be. We were able to visit one of the dorm rooms and my dad paid them the deposit so that I could have my own room. I loved the crisp clean air that I breathed. Juneau always brought me such joy. I knew getting a private room over shared rooms would be more expensive, but I hadn't had to share a bedroom in years, and I didn't want to start now. My sister and I always fought when we shared a room. My parents went as far as buying us a huge desk with shelves that were probably six feet tall and six feet long to give us our own space. Hers faced one direction and mine the other. With our beds on opposite side walls trying to make it like two separate rooms.

I always loved Juneau with every visit I made there to see my dad. If you can imagine a town sitting on picturesque mountains with the occasional snow cover. Water glistening in front of the town and yes, rain. A lot of rain, but the beauty masks the dreariness of the rain. In the summer when it was beautiful and sunny, you could see eagles flying all over. The waters full of salmon and streets bustling with tourists deboarding their fancy cruise ships hoping to catch all that Alaska has to offer. Growing up, I never understood why my mom didn't want to live here with my dad when the legislature was in session. He was a state senator, and every session lived in this beautiful city. We tried to live in Anchorage once so that we were at least closer to dad. That lasted less than a year. Mom loved Kotzebue and despised the rain. I never understood her hatred and sadness when it came to the rain. You could almost see the depression in her face when it started to drizzle.

"Excuse me sir, do you happen to know what time it is?" This handsome young man had these gorgeous eyes with the longest brown eye lashes. His darker eyebrows stood out to me. Realizing that this young man was looking for a reason to speak with me, my dad said, "I'm going to go pay our bill." We'd just finished breakfast at a restaurant in Anchorage and my dad was leaving me here with my sister Cheree to go to a concert that evening. The restaurant was one attached to a motel on 5th Street. I didn't understand why my dad wanted to go there but he said they had a good breakfast. It seemed a little dark and uninviting to me. However, breakfast was delicious. I found out the young man's name and I told him why I was in Anchorage. He said he was there trying to get into the Army. Then he said he would try to be at that concert and hoped to see me there.

That night I kept looking at the entrance even among the hundreds if not thousands who came in through the door, hoping I would see him walk through to no avail. It was odd that I could look at everyone's face who walked through and still not see his glimmering eyes through the crowd. I had hoped that I would be able to see him again.

MARRIAGE

I'm so nervous. Mom asked me over the phone who I was going to marry. I said, "You know, David, you met him when he drove from Juneau to Anchorage to meet you," My mom said anxiously, "Gee, if I knew you were going to marry him, I would have paid more attention to him." I quickly responded, "Mom, how many boyfriends have ever made a point of meeting you?" She agreed, not many.

I was so excited and scared at the same time. After all we hadn't known each other very long. I remember sitting in my single room reassuring my mom that all would be well. There were posters everywhere on my walls. And a mirror on the double closet doors. I kept looking at my reflection trying to reassure myself that all would be okay. It smelled as if one of my roommates was cooking breakfast. I thought to myself, 'how could you eat at a time like this?'.

My dad on the other hand had only one question, "Do you love him?" I assured him with a smile and happiness in my voice, "Yes, I do!" It was always easier to convince my dad of anything. My parents were apprehensive but knew they were not going to change my mind, as was the case all of my life.

Our wedding was simple. I was in my light pink dress that I wore to my junior prom. My mom had been so frustrated with me the year before because it took three and a half hours for me to find the perfect one and it was over three hundred dollars. I've been working since I was eleven years old. I reminded her that she hadn't bought my clothes for the last two years. She sighed and agreed. My sister complained none of her dresses were ever that expensive, but she and mom were thankful the three-and-a-half-hour ordeal was over. I thought this dress was perfect fitting and was happy with the lace arms, and lace over the whole dress.

Neither my family nor David's were present, for no other reason than finances. I told them that we were going to the justice of the peace anyway. Only Dean and Alice Diller were there and a friend from Kotzebue who happened to be going to the same college as me.

The justice of the peace's home was dark and dreary. I remember they didn't have any curtains open as it was winter. There was a lit Christmas tree in the corner, and I never noticed that we were standing under mistletoe. Not until I saw it in our wedding photos months later. We stood right next to their piano and said our vows. David was dressed in all black and looked cute as ever. He had a pink and white corsage, and I was holding a beautiful pink and white wedding bouquet. Both were made of carnations, that his mom ordered for us.

The house smelled a little musty, but I was so nervous and shy that I didn't really pay attention. I knew what I was getting into and always knew that marriage for me was the end. There is nothing else. I knew if and when I got married that it was a lifetime commitment. Even though I can tell you I had no idea how David felt about marriage. I believe we were just living in lust of the here and now.

FOUR DAYS TO WED

Dean and Alice Diller took David into their household as his twenty-four-seven sight and sound custodian with one goal in mind. Save this couple from ruin. You see, they knew we were getting married and I was not a Christian and David was. So that night we watched a Billy Graham movie. Alice was in her room praying for us, but we thought she wasn't feeling well.

Me; I related to the girl in this movie in every way. She was a partier and was living a hard life. The boyfriend strayed but was a Christian. This young couple were at a revival meeting where they begged people to come forward and accept Christ as their Lord and Savior. The boy did recommit his life to the Lord, and you could hear the girl's thoughts. She decided she would go forward, tomorrow.

The video ended with their car going off the edge of a cliff, a huge ball of fire and a very deep voice laughing and saying, "I got another one!" Well, like I said, throughout the entire video I related to this girl. So, it shook me to my core. I went into the kitchen shaking and David actually led me through the prayer of salvation. Me asking God to forgive me of my sins and accept me as His child. Thanking Christ for dying on the cross to take away my sins.

The kitchen was cold, and I remember shivering at the cold and at what I just witnessed. I cannot tell you how ecstatic Dean and Alice were. Dean was jumping up and down with tears rolling down his face and Alice just praising the Lord with her hands in the air and smiling ever so big. I felt a huge weight lifted off my shoulders. I had no idea that when you prayed this prayer and meant it with your whole being that you could feel so light and free. I felt like a whole new person with this hope. A feeling I cannot explain other than to say that years of deceit, lust, drinking, and helplessness was taken away from me.

The Diller's don't remember meeting David at Echo Ranch Bible Camp, but heard he attended as a boy. The camp is outside of Juneau on Berner's Bay. They heard he got into some trouble and needed a place to live and someone to watch over him. Without question, Dean just agreed to take David in. David was grateful but had no idea that when he was going to spend every waking hour with them, they would attend every service at the local church. David was just surprised that Dean never even spoke to Alice about it, just agreed yes, we'd take him in. Maybe they discussed it already, but who knows.

FELONY

On October 16, 1992, I was charged with Felony Aid and Abet. My lawyer worked out a deal and I was sentenced to Suspended Imposition of Sentence (referred to as an SIS in Alaska). This means upon satisfactory completion of probation it would be expunged from my record. No trace that it ever existed.

David was arrested at work, handcuffed and thrown into jail. Since we were in cahoots with each other we were given no visitation rights even though we were married. By this time, I was pregnant with our first, looking to raise him on my own. I know this seems abrupt and you would question, What? How? Why? Believe me, that is exactly what my parents thought too. David made some bad choices with an even worse 'friend' and they tried to rob this poor guy at gunpoint. David felt horrible immediately afterwards, but it was too late. I knew of the situation and even helped buy the nylons they wore on their heads to disguise themselves. But I never knew what it truly meant till it happened, and I broke it off with David. He told me it would never happen again and to please forgive him.

Once I began doing my court appointed Alcoholics Anonymous meetings and regularly checking in with my probation officer, David's lawyer made it so we could finally visit one another. David got to see our son probably a total of thirty hours of his first year and ten months of his life. I know it was of our own doing, but I will tell you it was one of the hardest times of my life. David was not present for our sons' birth. I was nineteen with a child and a husband who was in prison. My mom only stayed till our son was eighteen hours old. You see, there had been rain again the week of my son's birth and my mom just couldn't take it. She had to leave.

David and I - Lemon Creek Correction Center - Juneau - 1992

While David was at Lemon Creek Correctional Center, in Juneau, Alaska, I was all by myself with a newborn. I didn't have any money, but I was on Women Infant and Children (WIC) a government program that provides dairy and protein for pregnant women, or families with children toddler and under in age. I remember there were times that my dinner was peanut butter and saltine crackers. Most often my meals consisted of eating eggs and toast, three times a day. I remember my one-bedroom apartment, which was paid for through a government program as well. My walls and cupboards were bare. I didn't have any furniture; my mom and dad bought me a twin bed. I purchased a used couch from Goodwill. I cleaned it the best I could and kept a fitted sheet over it all the time.

When my mother-in-law, Lynda, came to visit after my son was born, she bought me a rocking chair and a crib. It was one of the loneliest times of my life. I remember sitting it that rocking chair trying to console my son when I couldn't even console myself. I missed David. I was nursing my son and kept having issues and I didn't have anyone around me to help. Even though I really desired to nurse my son I ended up switching to formula because WIC also paid for that as well.

When I went into the prison to visit David one of the guards asked me why I bothered wasting my time with him. He told me that I should just leave him. He said my husband would never change and he was not worth the wait. Even as hard as his sentence was on me and our marriage. I am thankful that I waited because our love was worth it. Nothing good in life comes easy.

BLESSED

David was finally granted parole – the only one for that quarter in the whole State of Alaska. One of many miracles we have been blessed with! You see, in order to have his parole granted he had to have a job and a place to live as soon as he got out. How can one get a job and have a place to live if he is in prison? By this time, I was living in Ketchikan, Alaska, where I was being supported by David's family. I met an amazing red-headed woman, Rebecca Mix, who took me under her wing and did one-on-one Bible studies with me. She always took time away from her family to take me out for tea or coffee. We would discuss the Bible and how life was going. She was the manager of an apartment building and wrote a letter to the parole board promising a place to live when David got out.

I contacted every place in Ketchikan asking for a job for my husband. Can you imagine getting a phone call, 'my husband is in jail, and I need to find him a job for when he gets out and you will need to write a letter to the parole board guaranteeing him a job.'

One of the local grocery store managers said he promised to hire him when he got out and wrote a letter to the board as well. All of this is so unheard of and again, one of many miracles, we were overcome with. It is hard to imagine even now. Sounds like a fairy tale, or perhaps a nightmare depending upon how you see it.

DESPERATION

After giving birth to my son and being alone for three months I couldn't handle it any longer. I was in Juneau and had no family. The friends that I had made were all college students still partying and living it up. I couldn't handle raising my son by myself any longer. Plus, the courts no longer would allow David and I to have face-to-face visits. This is one of the things that kept happening throughout his time in jail because even though we were married we had committed a crime together, so felons are not supposed to hang out. I told my husband that I was moving back to my hometown of Kotzebue, Alaska. My son knew it was an unhealthy move because this once very happy baby began crying all the time.

New Year's Eve. I decided to hire a babysitter and go out

and have fun. The very first party I ended up at I saw one of my brothers' best friends who I believed would care for me and allow me to 'live it up' so I asked him if he could drive for me. I got a smile and an eerie, "of course!" Well, that was my first mistake. And last time I would trust. I should have known better. My life had proved there were people that will fail you and take advantage of you. This would be one of the first times I went back to drinking. I wish I could say it was only this once but unfortunately, with my life choices, it would be the first of many.

Countless times I can remember when I felt scared or uncomfortable growing up. My first memory was needing to use the restroom. There were no lights on in the bathroom. That alone should have scared me. I could smell musty soap in the air. An elderly man who should have cared for me was taking a bath. He wanted me to touch him. The water was barely warm. I was maybe three years old and yet the memory is fresh as if it just occurred. I was so young I didn't understand what was happening, but I certainly knew I didn't feel okay about it. I wondered why this was happening and rushed to use the bathroom and get out of this despicable room.

Once when I was a grown woman, I confided in a close friend of my mom's saying I didn't understand the love my mom had for this elderly man. Her only response was you can't explain it to your mom because she probably already knows. I thought, "What? I still don't understand. What is this silence?"

This thought takes me back to a time I wanted to see what my mom would think and if she would support or help in any way, so I shared a story about a 'friend' and what happened to her on New Year's Eve. Her response was cold and unwavering. She said that my friend was ignorant for drinking and trusting. Her eyes were stern and a little distant.

I knew at that moment that I couldn't confide in her of the

constant occurrences in my life. Yes, constant. As if it is normal. Why do women think it is normal, or was it normal? Once I asked a female relative about three different male relatives and if they ever did such ugly things to her. She said no. Again, I feel I am all alone! How do they choose their victims?

I wanted to see what my female relative thought. It was cold outside, winter, and there was snow all over the ground. I asked her if she had ever been abused. She looked at me with a straight face and said, "No, why?" and I said, "I was just wondering if they ever messed with you too."

There was no more discussion. It was over, and implied that I was the one with the problem. The uneasiness reminds me of when one male relative in particular would be messing with me, I could hear his breathing in my ear, and it bothered me so. There are times when I am with my husband, and it takes me back to that same breath. I have to close my eyes and tell myself; this isn't ugly, this is with my husband, and it is meant to be beautiful. No one should ever be made to feel that its ugly or dirty.

There was a time when I was a pre-teen that my mom suspected something was going on. She asked me if this was the case. She had a stern look and wanted to know the truth because she suspected my male cousin. I was scared and I knew that I couldn't talk about such things, so I denied it until she believed me. I remember she came into my room smelling of alcohol and asked me. My room was disheveled as was our conversation. How can I speak of such ugliness? And if I did, would she say it was my fault. That I did something I should be ashamed of. It felt so cool in my room in that instant. I always wondered about the silence we were demanded to keep. It was like a hidden secret that no one should discuss of our relatives. That was one of the only times she brought it up, and I denied. Later, as years passed, I wished that I'd had the courage to say something. These were my secrets to keep, weren't they? I have since realized this is a generational curse.

REVELATION

My husband looked at my alarm clock for the very first time even though he used it probably a hundred times over our five and a half years of marriage, turning it off and on for work. He saw the *Damn Yankees* and *Bad Company* sticker on my alarm clock. He said, "Hey, I was going to go to that concert!" It was then that we realized that we actually met a year before we thought we met.

You see we thought we met the first time on September 18, 1991, at a party and never separated again till we married December 14, 1991. He was the handsome young man I was looking for at the concert clear back in March. I never got to tell my parents that it was us in that restaurant. I think my dad would have loved to hear that story. He would remember meeting him I'm certain. How many other coincidences would happen over the years? Even though I know there is no such thing. Everything happens for a reason, and God's will for our lives is so evident if you just look and listen.

David knows my past, and while it hurts him, it is a part of who I am and he loves me nonetheless. The only time we ever tried to live at home in Kotzebue was in 1995 and 96. We lasted a short nine months. We almost ended up separated. He up and quit his job at a local airline and bought a one-way ticket out of Kotzebue. He was leaving me and our two sons.

Life in the rural community and my family was too much for him. It has always been the same for me. David did not like when I was around my family because he says I turn into someone different. Someone who has something to prove. I have only been back a hand full of times, and as much as it hurts, I can't go back. I have never felt safe there. I don't belong. I'm an outsider. David was convinced he could have been the last one on the plane that day and they would still be announcing, "We are full and need a volunteer to deboard the plane. We will reissue this ticket and one more to use at a future date." Reluctantly, he finally got off the plane and came home and told me. We left Kotzebue as a family eleven days later.

He was one of the only people I knew who stood up to my mother. My mom while she tolerated him, didn't like him because he didn't like the way she spoke to me or what he says is the 'Kagoona' way (my mother's maiden name). To pretend something didn't happen and therefore it didn't.

That reminds me of a time when I was a junior in high school. I left the house and was staying with a friend when my mom's drinking got heavy. I didn't want to be there because it could get ugly. I left and spent the night out with my best friend. My mom called and told me I could not stay but I was not going to go home. Later that evening, my dad drove my mom to my friend's house, and she drug me out of the house by my hair. I have never hit my mom, and I never would because I knew it was the alcohol and her past that frightened us so. I stood up, pushed her down to the floor and ran out of the house.

I stayed at another friend's house for three days. I wasn't going to go home, she had to know I'd had enough. When I came into the house three days later, I was a little worried and scared of what might be waiting for me. I walked in the door, she came out of her room and said, "Hi babe, there's food in the fridge." That was it. Nothing was ever said again.

I went to school with a friend for the first half of my senior year to get away from her drinking. I lived in Soldotna. I once again convinced my dad that I needed to get away and that it would prepare me to live away from home once I go off to college. He agreed and I got to go. Soldotna was not the best move for me. But it did allow me to live away from my mom and Kotzebue.

While I was in Soldotna, I did a lot of drinking. One of our friends was living nearby in Kenai so we would get together almost every weekend and drink. That was when I first moved there. Later, I would fly to Anchorage to see my sister, because it was only a half-hour plane ride. One night I even drove drunk. I am so thankful nothing bad happened. One, I should not have been drinking and driving and am ever so thankful it did not end in tragedy. Two, I cannot drive a stick shift to save my life, and yet I did. Finally when we got to my friends' house in Kenai me and a friend, needed to pee so bad that we jumped out of the car and peed right there in the parking lot. Our friends' mom said, "Yeah, I thought I heard you girls get here and I look out the window and here are two moons looking at me."

I'm thankful that in the midst of all my poor choices God was looking out for me and ensured that nothing worse happened even though it should and could have. Another time I did this was when I moved back to Kotzebue for the other half of my senior year. I wanted to graduate with my classmates. We had our graduation party and that evening I had another person that I asked to drive me everywhere. The night is a blur but when I came to the next day, I for the first time in my life awoke from my drunken stupor and I was behind the wheel and stuck in the mud. My friend was helping me get un-stuck. It is a scary feeling to come to and find yourself behind a wheel. I wouldn't wish that on anyone.Those were two very careless mistakes that I made when I was young and foolish. Again, I am thankful they did not end in tragedy.

DEATH

My sister, Charlene and I, began getting the brunt of my mom's drunken stupors, after a horrific event that sent my brother off to prison for the next several years. That is not my story to tell other than to say the song *"We are the World"* by USA for Africa, had just come out. My friend and I listened to it on repeat that whole year. I just started the eighth grade. My life went in a way I wasn't prepared for. The reason that the song meant so much at the time the world was trying to raise money for food for starving children in Africa. It was the desperation of someone in need. At that time, I needed my brother. He protected me from my mom. I changed when he went to prison. My whole family changed. My mom's heart couldn't take it. My brother was in and out of prison for years. My aches and pains grew both literally and figuratively. I love my mother, but things got so much harder. I learned so much about pain, disappointment and heartache. A piece of me died.

PEDESTAL

After leaving Alaska in 1996, we found out I was pregnant with baby number three. With each child we moved further south. One was born in Juneau, Alaska, another in Ketchikan, Alaska and one in Port Angeles, Washington. Six and a half months after we left Kotzebue. I was doing a ladies Bible study in my home. David, who was working fourteen-to-sixteen-hour days six days a week, went to a men's conference, Promise Keepers, where he rededicated his life to the Lord.

He felt convicted that if he wanted his children to feel church was important then it had to be important to him as well. What

I didn't know was that he also made his own personal deal with God. If she asks just like this, I will tell. Right before my Bible study was to begin, I asked him just so. He hesitantly shared with me that he'd been unfaithful to me with a call girl on one of his visits to Anchorage. I instantly felt anguish for this woman and what she had put herself through to allow this horrific exchange.

Of course, that is not a normal human response, the only way to describe it is that it came from the Lord. You see, I had put David on a pedestal. He knew what I went through as a child and then as an adult. I knew he would never hurt me in this way. Through much counseling and prayer and seeking of forgiveness on both parts I know no one deserves that pedestal but Christ Himself.

Believe me there were times I was angry at God for giving me compassion and yet it reminds me of another time. You know, my father was one of the greatest men I knew. He loved all four of us sibling in such a way that each one of the four of us felt as though we were his favorite. Even though I know without a doubt that my siblings are all wrong and I was his favorite. What a blessed gift.

ANGUISH

Here is my prayer list for March 15, 1998:

1. Show respect to my husband
2. Stop swearing
3. Daily prayers and devotions
4. Recover from miscarriage
5. Be a Godly mother and wife
6. Help financially

I've been married over thirty-one years and I'll tell you; I'm still working on number one. Now number two, I like. This is always a struggle... not as bad as some. Trust me, I'm no Samuel L Jackson, I'm not crude mostly it is when I stub my toe or break something. Almost get in an accident. Nothing vulgar. I always tell people, "I'm not as bad as my sister, Cheree. She'd make a sailor blush!" I love the other prayer requests, but what I'm going to talk about is number four; recover from miscarriage. I was three and a half months pregnant when David and I lost our fourth child. That was so very hard on us. I remember when I first found out I was pregnant I was not happy or excited.

You see, my daughter was born early in 1997, these two were going to be so close in age. Much of my early pregnancy I worried about how we were going to afford another child, how I was going to have four children under six years of age. It was a lot for both of us. When I had my miscarriage, I truly believed it was because of my negative thoughts and all that goes with that. We had just started to pick out names and finally started getting excited. The emotional and physical strain that goes on with your body and mind are so extreme. I know without a doubt that someday we will have a reunion with this child in heaven. I have often wondered if past decisions chose this outcome.

UTTER LOSS

June 5, 2003, was one of the worst days of my life and yet, the most blessed hope! My sister Cheree, who to me is one of the strongest Eskimo women, I know, next to my mother. She made it so that I could fly all the way to Kotzebue from Omaha, Nebraska, to say goodbye to my dad. She had done the resuscitation on my dad who suffered his fourth stroke at our family camp, Aki (pronounced: a-key), below Noorvik, and was choking on breakfast. She performed CPR until help arrived at the camp thirty-five minutes later. I prayed and prayed I would get there in time. When I landed in Anchorage I stayed at my aunts' house. She had given me an alarm clock so I could wake up early to catch the first flight to Kotzebue. The alarm clock was the old wind-up kind. I prayed and prayed all night long that the tick of every second was my dad's heartbeat. Thanks to my sister, who never gave up, I got to see him. Before he passed away, he awoke long enough to say, "Crystal." I told him I loved him. My mom and sisters and some of the other people in my dad's room went out to smoke a cigarette and I was finally alone except for one elderly man. I desperately wanted to be alone with my dad but finally called out to him when they left.

When he passed, my sisters, my mother and I surrounded his body. I saw him take his last breath and watched as a tear rolled down his face. Immediately I saw the blessed hope that Christians have and the utter loss when Christ is not a part of your life. My sisters were hysterical. Don't get me wrong, as I already said he was the greatest man I knew. But immediately I heard so loud it was almost deafening, "When peace like a river, attendeth my way," and yet it was so calm and assuring that it wasn't loud at all. If you are not familiar with it please look up the hymn *It is Well with my Soul* by: Philip Paul Bliss and Horatio G. Spafford so you get all the words; because I heard the whole hymn. That was the peace I received from God when I questioned my sympathy for the other woman. God promises this kind of peace to all who repent and ask Him to be their Savior. It will come in the most horrific times of your life, and it will surpass all understanding!

OMAHA

David and I ended up in Omaha, Nebraska, because of Dean and Alice, they recommended Grace University. From the moment they mentioned it, I heard Grace, and I felt it in my soul, it was where we were supposed to be. I hounded David until he finally agreed to call them. He spoke with a student, admissions counsellor, over the phone and he instantly felt a call to be there as well.

There are so many blessings I can tell you that happened there, like me making the best friends I have ever had in my life. There is a group of six woman who I met with once a month for years, we would eat a meal together, and play games. Laughing and having the best time. We prayed for each other. We went through a house fire together, a divorce, becoming a widow, health deterioration and laughter, so much laughter. Even miles apart whenever we get together it is as though we haven't been apart. David and I were given couches, loveseats, beds from different families and the furniture matching as if we bought them together. Another time we did not have any food and a couple people showed up with a Thanksgiving feast to feed an army. We had instructors who truly cared about us and encouraged our spiritual growth.

While in Omaha I led a break out session at a ladies' retreat on the power of prayer. When I entered the classroom, I saw all older, grey-haired ladies, much wiser women and I thought to myself, 'What am I doing teaching these women.' I remember praying, "Please Lord give me the words," and guess what? He did. Just like when I led Bible studies. If you are willing and pray earnestly for the Lord to use you, He will. I simply shared how the Lord was faithful in every situation. I shared examples of some very real requests and His answers. I encourage you to keep a prayer log or journal. If you don't write them down, how will you know when He answers them. The point is, He will be there for you if you again, look and listen, write it down so you have proof.

David and I shared in youth ministry, and I did woman's ministry for sixteen years of our children's lives. We mentored a lot of youth over the years. Made many mistakes but loved and cherished our times. David and I struggled in our thirty-one years of marriage as all couples do. With us it was infidelity on both parts and my drinking to hide the pain I felt inside. But one thing that has remained constant is our love for each other. Our love for our kids and the constant love and forgiveness we've been blessed with by Christ. Like the fact that we are still together. We have four grandchildren now who we adore.

PRAYING

When our youngest was just born, I used to climb my backyard fence and quietly enter the back entrance of my neighbor's house. It led into her kitchen. Often Carmen had tea or coffee waiting for me. At the time my husband was working so many hours six days a week. Carmen and I took turns praying for our families trusting the Lord to protect our hard-working husbands. If my newborn was asleep when the alarm went off, I would let her sleep in our room with her dad. But if she was awake, I bundled her up and took her with me. We spent probably three days a week doing this. There were days I was so exhausted Carmen always told me if I was too tired to sleep in and she understood. But often I would lay in bed feeling guilty that she would be there alone so I would get up and make myself go and pray not just because it was the right thing to do but I was so blessed by our time on our knees asking the Lord to watch over our loved ones.

And thanking him for another day to live and love some more. Every good thing that was in our life. I prayed for my children and their future spouses. I prayed continuously that they would find true love to spend the rest of their lives worshipping our Lord together.

GLIMPSES

I go back to the hints of seeing God's goodness in our lives like when we were leaving Tempe, Arizona and I met a lady who knew my mother from the forced boarding school that she and countless other Alaska Natives had to go to. We were having a garage sale and she came to see what we were selling. I wish I could remember her name, but I don't. Anyway, she was at my garage sale with her granddaughters. She looked at me and asked if I was Alaska native and I told her yes, I was an Inupiaq from Kotzebue. She asked me where my mom was from, and I told her Noorvik. Then she asked me what her maiden name was, and she said she knew her. They didn't get to stay for too long, but it was so good to see someone all the way in Arizona that knew my mother. Even if it was for only a very brief moment.

This led me to think about what my mom went through as a child. I can tell you about the many oppressed families that got separated because they had to go to school elsewhere because rural schools only went to elementary. Imagine a pre-teen child forced to leave their home. Their way of life. All you have known. To go off to an unknown place. For my mom, she was sent to Mt. Edgecumbe in Sitka, Alaska where it rains 131.74 inches annually and thirty-three inches of snow for most of two-hundred and fifty-two-days out of the year. This happened to my mom and countless others just as they are at the age of getting into their menstrual cycles. No family. At first, no friends. I realize this is one of the reasons rains depressed my mother so. But I will also say this is what made her so strong. She was one of the strongest Inupiat women I knew. She met her best friend from Barrow there too. Life-long friends, like no one could understand. We only understood a small portion of what their relationship meant to each other. My mom had so much pain and suffering in her life, but you never knew what she was really thinking or feeling until she drank. Then we got glimpses of her struggle, but only just.

DESOLATE

My mom was among the hundreds of Natives that were put in a box, painted black on the inside so no light would shine in, simply for speaking in their Native tongue. This happened at school all the time. And much worse. Many of these teachers were missionaries sent to 'teach' us the proper way of living. I know so many in my mom's generation that turned their backs on God because what kind of a God is this that would allow such oppression? I know many became Christians but the tragedies they'd seen...

Then the time a young man showed up at my house in Phoenix to install my T.V. and he just happened to be from Selawik, Alaska where my dad was born. You could just feel our pride and strength when we realized there were two of us Alaska Natives under the same roof. David walked in the door and wondered what he had missed because we're both sitting in the living room with smiles on our faces. I told him this guy is from Selawik, he was shocked, "Really? What brought you all the way from there to here?" He said that he joined the military right after school as a way to escape life from there. He went back for his Ahnas' funeral a year back but that was the first and last time he returned. I feel as though all of us Alaska Natives have had to find strength to survive or become defeated. I have always chosen to be stronger. Be bolder, be more. My strength comes from the Lord, and all I learned from my mom and dad.

I have never blamed my mom or my dad for anything. I knew they did the best that they could with what they had. There were times when my children were growing up that I drank too much and was hard on them. But I too, did the best I could with what I was given. If I had it to do over again, I would want to be a mother like my daughter, Hailey, is to her children. She is patient, loving and kind, and has taught her children to have a voice.

I know now my mom faced many demons and overcame a lot of them. She had such a peaceful passing. We were in her room and she died with peace in her heart and a sweet smile on her face. I am thankful for both my mom and my dad. They were great people who served many. My house was never empty. Mom would feed everyone who walked through the door. And many came unexpectedly but were always welcomed to a warm house, and great food. I didn't understand as a child that this wasn't a normal thing. There was hardly a meal at our house that didn't include at least one guest. My sister Charlene asks me all the time, "Do you remember when, (*insert name*) lived with us?" I don't remember anyone living with us except my three siblings and my parents, but apparently, my mom and dad also housed many people in our home. I remember my cousins that would come in for doctor appointments, or shopping and stuff like that but not really anyone that stayed for long periods of time. Anyway, that was who they were. They welcomed anyone and everyone.

MY DAD

So many called him a great storyteller. And he was. I remember when we would go to camp, he would entertain all the kids and tell us stories till we went to sleep. Silly stories, funny stories, and scary stories too. One story he told stood out to me because he was always very animated as he told a story.

"Once upon a time there was a giant, and with each step he took the whole ground would shake." He would put his arms out making a big half circle and stomp his feet with a wide stance making a loud grunting noise as he took steps. He even included villages. If a child was from Noorvik, he would talk about the giant would take one step from Kotzebue and the other step all the way to Noorvik. He made their home feel special. He would go to each child and ask us, "Are you, (insert name) – he would take turns with each child that was listening to the story. One by one they would say no, and he would get to the final child, and they would say, "Yes." And he would say, "Are you a pooper!" Of course, every child would love that story. They get to be the main character and then it ended with something that made all little kids laugh. Which of course would lead to the adults laughing. He just had a way to include everyone and for everyone to feel special.

My family was the most blessed because during the school year and the holidays that come during that time, we spent it with my dad's side of the family. We spent most of the summertime with my mom's side of the family. All the things you imagine about Alaska. We spent the summers on planes, and in boats traveling to our family campsites, swimming in the rivers. In the winter we took snow machines and cars and drove everywhere. We went sledding and skiing and occasionally dog sledding.

I often look at pictures of my dad and the man he was. At a young age he knew what he was supposed to do and how he would help others. My cousin Roberta told me that her dad and our uncles were so mad when he chose to let his private pilot license go. You see, these three brothers were pilots as was the man who raised them. I didn't even know that my dad was a pilot. As soon as my dad won the State Representative seat he told them, he could only focus on that now.

Dr. Oliver Leavitt a leader and pioneer for Barrow and the surrounding area asked me when I came home for my dad's funeral. "Did I ever tell you the story of why I supported your father?" I told him, "No!" He said my wife kept telling me, you need to fly to Kotzebue to meet and hear my best friends' husband. He said she kept bugging him and kept bugging him, relentlessly. He finally said, "You make the arrangements." He said he met my dad and knew he was the right man for the job. He called his other constituent in Barrow and said, "You're going to have to find a new campaign manager because I have a new constituent." He told me that my dad won his first representative seat as a write-in. My father accomplished so much and even more than I can tell you as a representative for the very fortunate

Northwest Alaskan residents. I remember hearing a story about former mayor Byron Mallott, from Yakutat he said he could not get funding or approval for a pool in their community. My dad told him he was going about it all wrong and told him that he needed to present it as a backup water reservoir for the fire department. It was approved.

His lifelong aide and friend, Mike Scott said that he knew the art of the deal. And he did. My dad knew how to find a way to better everyone's life. He was an incredible servant. He took his job and responsibility seriously. He knew he represented the people. He never took that for granted or lightly. He hardly slept, usually three to six hours a night with sometimes two to three ten to thirty-minute cat naps a day. One of my favorite photos of him is him sleeping on the couch in his office in Juneau. His fingers are crossed together on his chest as if he's praying.

My sister Cheree and I shared a bedroom till our two older siblings left the house. When we were young, we had a bunkbed and at night we prayed together. I would get on my knees, and my sister who had the top bunk would put her knees on my shoulders and we would pray together. Even now, I can see it… that is such a beautiful symbol.

When I reached out to Mike to let him know I was writing this book, this is what he said about my father, "What a cool hard-nosed but humble public servant. Unique in Alaska history. Nobody like him before and still nobody since. His mastery of the Alaska legislative process was unequaled in my experience."

When my father passed away, they listed his achievements on the back of his obituary. The list was long. But I want to give you an idea, so you see what I mean. The man was amazing in his own right. Here are just a few. 1. Brought live television to the State of Alaska. 2. Brought the telephone to all the bush communities. 3. Funding construction and maintenance of the rural schools. 4. Established Barrow and Kotzebue courts. 5. Led efforts to establish the rural housing assistance loan program, which led to commercial renting in rural Alaska. 6. University of Alaska rural Education and facilities programs. 7. Establishing the village health aid program and rural clinic to provide a resident health care practitioner in every village. Just to name a few. He made it so students could go to school at home. He made it so I could go to school at home. I'm thankful that I did not have to go to a new place as a small child. I got to stay home with my family, and still get an education. People were allowed basic health care in their villages and people in Northwest Alaska were allowed to be tried in their own hometowns as opposed to being sent to court miles and miles away from home.

Whenever I tell people my dad was a politician, I say he was not a typical politician. He worked hard for the people and never rested until their lives were for the better. When I was young my dad got a DUI driving in Anchorage. I remember he was so embarrassed and ashamed; he didn't let it end there. He stopped drinking. On his own, just stopped and focused on helping people. I remember Mike would ride in the car alongside my dad who ran next to it, getting healthier. My dad was the perfect example. Mistakes do not define you, what you learn and apply from those mistakes is what defines you.

MY MOM

My mom was a leader and servant in her own right. She had twin boys between my brother Duane and my sister Charlene. Marvin and Martin. She never talked about them. As far as I know, no one did. One boat ride she just casually said, that is where my sons are buried. What? That is when I found out that she had twins, and one died at birth the other three months later. They couldn't do for preemies then, what they can now. I'm certain with memories that still haunt, she was on the school board for sixteen of my school years. She fought for the students and paved the way for growth. I always knew education was important. From the time I was little, while others played house or whatever other little girls did. I played school. All my stuffed animals were students. I had books everywhere. And I was reading aloud to them. I wanted my children to know that education is important to me, so the year after my eldest graduated high school I got my Bachelor of Science degree in English Education. Then while I was working at American Airlines in Arizona, I got my master's in business administration.

My mom worked at the local bank and at the housing authority. My parents played a huge role into who I am today. Serving and honoring others. My mom would often tell me how good she was at math. We butted heads a lot. I had a hard time thinking of how she contributed to who I am, and I think it was her strength and her attitude. The winter that my father passed away my mom was determined to go hunting alone. When my dad was alive, they often went with her sister and her husband. They offered to go on this one, but mom, knew her life was on her own now. So, she hopped on the snowmachine, and took off to hunt for moose all on her own. She came home several hours later and called for my brother to help her take it off the sled. That was the type of woman she was. None of the four of us siblings learned how to speak Inupiaq, she loved the fact that she could talk around us and none of us understood her secrets.

As an adult now I think back to when we were at camp, and she would make these incredible meals. Here we are at camp, sometimes just on a river bar and she would make steaks and potatoes with onions and asparagus this incredible, extravagant meal while we are camping. She made it over a campfire. She made life seem easy. One time we were so embarrassed because she changed her top right in front of the window with no bra, at a hotel in Anchorage. She said, "What? I don't have anything anyone hasn't already seen." She didn't care. She was who she was and didn't care what anyone thought. She loved to laugh. She had a beautiful laugh.

HUNTING

One caribou season when I was about eight years old. We were at our camp Aki, everyone said they went up to the look-out tower and saw caribou. Our lookout tower was amazing, it was such a tall tower. It made it so you can see all the game around you. I was busy doing my own thing but was upset that I did not get the opportunity to see them. Like everything else when you're the youngest you think you're missing out. I tried to get someone to go with me but they were too excited, the caribou were on the way and it was time to get some fresh meat in the freezer.

Young and mad little me, I chose to climb that tall tower on my own so I could see them. It was a straight up and down ladder made of poles from the local trees. I climbed up and looked for all I could. I never saw a thing. I came down upset that yet again I missed out. While I was climbing down, the ladder began to shake, and I truly thought there was an earthquake. When I finally got to the bottom as quick as I could, I realized the earthquake was hundreds of caribou running right next to the lookout. I hadn't seen them because they were beneath me. Even in this it is hard to describe. Can you imagine having hundreds of caribou running so close to you that you think you're having an earthquake? This is one of the many blessings I had growing up. We lived an Eskimo fairy tale.

Another memory I have is my dad taking me seal hunting. I only remember one trip. It was just my dad and I and we had finally, after what seemed like forever, spotted a seal. My dad had been practicing shooting with me prior so I had become a pretty good shot. He said, now when that seal comes up out of this hole, I'll shoot it and then you can take a shot. Snow and ice covered everything, and it seemed to take forever. But I was a little girl so who knows how long it really was. Well, when I spotted the seal I thought, 'he just wants to take the credit for shooting it instead of me,' So I shot. I hit it but the seal dove back through the hole and got away. My dad had a real rifle that would have killed the seal. I had a simple .22. The biggest lesson I learned is my dad's patience. He never got angry with me. He just said, "I was going to shoot it first." And I smiled and said, "You just wanted to say you shot it." He smiled back and said, "Yeah, but you got it." I thought he was trying to take something away from me, and I felt like all my life that is what happens… something gets taken from me or I don't get to participate for one reason or another, so I chose otherwise. Not knowing that I was just hurting the seal and letting it get away damaged.

Our native way of life is so unheard of and people usually get grossed out when they hear about the delicacies' we've eaten all of our life. If you research it, we've had sunglasses far longer than in the western world. Our clothing came from the animals we've eaten. We use every part of an animal for meals, clothing, tools… you name it, our ingenuity is incredible. We learned how to survive in 60 below. Our igloos for hunting were temporary shelter to keep the cold wind and chilly temperatures away from our bodies.

We eat whale, seal, moose, caribou, goose, duck, you name it. And when we hunt, our first kill of any animal whether from land, air or sea goes to an elder. We were taught to respect our elders. It is ingrained in us from the time we are born. They have the knowledge. They have lived here longer. They suffered many atrocities yet overcame them all. Our elders represent knowledge and power. They teach us right from wrong.

GAMES

My family played so many games growing up. We played Norwegian, a baseball like game that we just ran all over and competed against each other. Red rover, sending one person over to run through the line we made by holding hands and they had to run through and break our arms. We played Sorry, Aggravation, Monopoly, Snirts, which is like Dutch blitz only with a regular deck of cards. And so many other games. The adults would all play together at one table and the kids at another. We played games challenging everyone. Me being the youngest I almost always got left out so I did what I could to be able to compete. If it was a dice game, they said I took too long to add up the numbers, so I quickly learned when I rolled to just move my piece each number of the die, so I didn't have to count. So, if it was a seven, I moved three, then four, so I didn't count the total just each individual die so I was always right, but they didn't have to wait for me to add it up.

Every time I played a game, that is what I did. I learned ways to be quick enough so I would be included but it was not always the proper way. Just like learning to swim, my dad threw me into the river right in front of our camp in Aki. All my cousins and siblings were swimming, so when he did that. It truly was a sink or swim moment. I learned to swim. I'm thankful for my dad doing that because even as an adult today, I think I will either sink or swim and if nothing else, die trying. That is my motivation when I work, when I play, anything and everything I do. I want to strive and do my best. I want to swim.

NAÏVE

Yes, I was very naïve growing up. Not about some things I suppose but I remember stealing cigarettes as a nine-year-old from my parents or from their friends. Nine years old, are you joking? No, you see. I come from a big family. When I say big, I'm not kidding. On my mom's side of the family there were nineteen first cousins and on dad's there were twenty-one first cousins. I was the youngest on my dad's side of the family and second youngest on my mom's side. Well, the family that lived close. Two cousins which were younger, lived in Anchorage. All that to say, I wanted to be like the big cousins and that is where I learned to steal cigarettes and later to smoke marijuana. I started smoking both at a very young. As an adult I kind of laugh but am ever so grateful I can tell people I smoked cigarettes, heavily and frequently from age nine to eighteen. When I found out I was pregnant with my eldest I quit smoking. It was that easy, and I am thankful. I know many who suffer and cannot quit. It should have been harder, but I had a life in me, and it was easy.

By high school I was already drinking and smoking both cigarettes and marijuana on a regular basis. Me and one of my new friends said we were sleeping at each other's' house with the full intent to drink and hang out with another friend who was living on her own with a boyfriend.

We were drinking and smoking, and my friend pulled out these dehydrated mushrooms. Everything I am about to tell you, me and my friend still agree happened. Me and my new friend had no idea what they were. No joking. Naïve I know, but we had no idea. She just said, "Really, they're good, you'll like them." So, we took them. As soon as her boyfriend came home, he was furious that she shared it with us, and I told my friend that he looked like the devil. She agreed. We began walking to my house. The entire town of Kotzebue folded on fifth street (one of the main streets in our town) and in our stupor, everyone in the town was watching us walk home to my house.

It felt like it took forever to get there, even though our town is tiny and at the very most should take a half hour to walk from one end to the other. We finally made it to my house. We went up the stairs to my bedroom. As soon as I entered my room, I turned off the lights and instantly we were both lost even though my room was tiny. It was the smallest room in the house, the size of a large closet. Once the lights turned out we couldn't find our way. We finally crawled our way to my bed and both of us were lying in bed and we couldn't speak. We were talking, but our lips weren't moving. After what seemed like forever all of a sudden, we were at our funerals. We both could hear people talking about us and why we would ever do such a thing. We were so ashamed and scared and in terror. We both believed we were at our funerals and being buried alive. We could hear them, but we could not yell loud enough. Needless to say, we never did that again.

SHAME

My first serious boyfriend began with me deceiving and manipulating my best friend from kindergarten. We were the best of friends, inseparable for more than eight years. But he liked me better, at least that was my excuse. She dodged a bullet if I do say so myself. Together we were wannabe pot-dealers, enough to support our habit anyway. He beat me on several occasions and for whatever reasons I stayed with him. I kept going back to him. I got pregnant at a very young age from a relationship that never should have been. I was way too scared to tell my mom. And I didn't want to see the disappointment in my dad's face. So, I did the next worse thing. I called one of my mom's closest friends, "I'm too scared to tell my mom," She just said, "Oh, Crystal!" Well, she must've been too scared too because it took her forever to tell my mom.

By the time I went to Anchorage to see a doctor to have an abortion it was almost too late. I cannot tell you the pain and anguish I felt. It hurt and smelled like nothing else I can describe. The sounds alone haunt my dreams. I remember the doctor coming out and telling my mom and dad, "Well, she is farther along than you said, so it is taking longer," I cried. Even with all of this, I kept going back to him. I don't know how many times we broke it off then went back to each other. One of my childhood classmates came to me and said, "I'm so glad you finally broke up with him," and she proceeded to tell me that he was unfaithful to me when I was in the hospital with a broken leg. That is when it finally hit me. In my weakest, I wasn't worthy so finally, neither was he. After that I had a few relationships off and on but when one of them started to get too serious, I left. I knew I didn't want to live in Kotzebue. So even if I had some serious and real relationships, I knew I was not going to stay, so I ended it, most often, not very nicely. I am looking forward to meeting my baby in heaven someday.

When I was finally single as a junior in high school, I joined volleyball. Basketball was always my sister's Cheree's thing, and she was good at it, until our broken legs. I loved building a comradery with these girls. I was so excited to be a part of something again. I enjoyed it so much I wished I played sooner. We made it to regionals in Nome and I even had an article written in the *Arctic Sounder* that spoke of the solid serves from Ferguson. I had found something else I was good at and I loved it. I remember the movie *Ghost*, by Bruce Joel Rubin, had just come out and right before our game the Nome volleyball girls loaned us the movie. We got to watch just over half the movie then it was time to start our game. We beat them. We were headed to State. I cannot tell you how excited we all were. We were yelling and screaming and cheering. After we beat them, we went to finish the movie and the girl that loaned it took it back. We never got to finish it.

COMPETE

By eleven years old I was going to the teen center dances and have so much fun. One year I even competed in a dance competition with a great partner. I remember one by one other couples falling left and right being tagged out of the competition. I started getting nervous when it came down to about four couples. I looked at my partner, "I'm the youngest one here!" he eased my anxiety and said "Keep going, you got this!" We came in second place. I was so very excited and happy. I love competing. Doesn't matter if it is a game, a race, a ride. Whatever.

For my thirteenth birthday I was drinking, and a very tough and extremely scary person threatened to beat me. I honestly, don't know why. I waited until I saw my sister Charlene and I told her Tami Stevens threatened to beat me. Charlene said she would have a talk with her. So glad I told my sister. Even though if you met her, you would see, she is all of four-foot-eleven maybe. If she stands tall anyway. Tami was taller and stronger in every way you could imagine.

Years later talking to Tami, she said, "Charlene scared her to death and that she would never touch me or my sister Cheree". Charlene, while small, can truly carry her own. When she was in high school, she competed in the Native Youth Olympics (NYO). Strength and endurance competitions where competitors compete against each other for events like stick pull, two opponents place their feet sole to sole and you place a stick about the size of a broom stick, but not as long and they tug and pull without separating their feet until someone is either lifted off the ground or one opponent rips the stick out of the others hand. The entire time your hands have to stay closed and not lose a grip. There are all kinds of different events like that. Each event represents different aspects of our culture. Meaning the event built our strength for survival.

My sister, Charlene, competed in the leg competition. It is where two opponents lay on the ground heads in opposite direction. The opponents lie with their hips side by side and the leg closest to each other lifts into the air and they basically tap their ankles in the air above them and then lower their legs to the ground three times while counting aloud. On the third count, they wrap their knees together, and your back must stay on the ground, and you try to flip your opponent over using your legs only. Your hands must clasp together on your stomach and your elbow closest to your opponent wraps around theirs and must not come undone either. Whoever flips the other person over wins. I told you how tall Charlene was but most all her life she has also been about 118 pounds. She was able to beat all of her competitors and won at state.

I remember feeling like I dodged a bullet when Charlene stepped in for me with Tami. I went into the dance and danced my heart out... until I was told I needed to leave because they could tell I had been drinking. I was bummed. They said they were sorry, and said, "Hey by the way, what birthday is this?" and I smiled and said, "My thirteenth!" and that is when they knew I had been going for two years before I was supposed to.

My sister Cheree was competing with everyone in dance as well, but her dancing was far different. She picked up break dancing. I don't know from where, but she was very good at it. Constantly someone would challenge her because she had beat all her competitors. No one could, she was good and would win every challenge that was thrown her way. Some of the guys were pretty hurt they were being beat by a girl, but she could do it all, and dressed the part. She could do the wave, the worm, the moonwalk, every move out there, she was good at it.

Lance Kramer, a pastor in Kotzebue, helped me to understand more about NYO. He leads a children's camp outside of Kotzebue where children from all over the region get to hear about Jesus. He was my sister Cheree's classmate. He still raises his children in Kotzebue and now he and Corina have two granddaughters. He hunts, fishes and traps there. He has also passed down all of it to each one of his children and teaches the students no matter what he is doing. Lance said there were three types of games. Ones that build flexibility and agility, like one- and two-foot-high kick, the Alaskan high kick, and the scissor broad jump. He said this helps us with our speed and agility like when we have to hop from ice flow to ice flow to get to a piece of ice that our dead ugruk (seal) in on. Pain games help us to push past the pain and deliver regardless of circumstance. When we are hunting it is for survival for our families at home to eat. We have to push through the cold fingers, the cramped toes, sitting for hours. These games are the ear pull, the wrist carry and the seal hop. Finally, there are strength games like the Indian stick pull, Eskimo stick pull, kneel jump and leg wrestling. Lance equated the stick pull with needing to pull a heavy seal into your boat. You must use your legs, your back, everything to get it into the boat.

All our NYO games build our muscles for a real purpose. Each event represents something that we must do physically to continue to feed and clothe our families. When I was in high school, I wanted to go to Anchorage and compete in our Olympics as well. I looked at all our different games and wondered what I could compete and win in. I chose the seal hop. Lance said that it is considered a pain game. No kidding. For women, we lie in a push up position, never bending more than a ninety-degree angle with your arms and you hop never arching your back, all the way down the gym. For the men it is far more painful, they must do the same thing only on their knuckles. Well, when I competed, I had to beat out my competition, so I did. I proceeded to go the length of the gym and about a quarter of the way back. I was going. Sadly, when I got to Anchorage, I was so embarrassed when I saw all the students that were watching me that I went about four feet and stopped. I'm sad now of course that I did that, but back then I just saw it as a way to get out of Kotzebue for free.

SUSTENANCE

When I was about seven years old, we went to our camp Aki, I remember my family really wanted to catch a sii fish (Alaskan white fish, pronounced *shee* fish). My cousin Sadie was with us. I remember we were out on the ice in front of Aki ice fishing in the lake. We had dug a hole in the ice and were trying to catch another one of our many delicacies, our yummy sii fish. No one was catching anything, and we really wanted it for our dinner that evening. Everyone was giving up but apparently even as a child I didn't give up easily.

As I was raising my hand-made ice fishing rod, think of a boomerang with the straight edge with a caved divot so on each end the fishing line wraps around and around making a long oval. This is our ice fishing rod. You release the fishing line into the water and continuously pull the rod up in the air with a jerking motion. This mimics the movement of a live thing swimming for the fish to bite into.

I thought I felt a nibble and I very well could have. So here I am trying to pull the string to reel the fish in. By this time some adults came to help me. Turns out I was stuck on the bottom so the adults walked away. Well, I wasn't going to give up so I pressed on. Jerking that fishing line desperate to reel a big one. When all of a sudden there was tugging. I announced it and of course the adults didn't believe me. Finally, my cousin Sadie came over and yelled, "She does!" and she and I preceded to pull and pull on the fishing line. We had gloves on so it did not hurt us but Eskimo fishing rods are far different than the modern ones. I told you to think of a boomerang, but you have to wrap the fishing line back around to make the long narrow oval to make a straight edge out of the boomerang. So, you're pulling in the fishing line with your hands until you reel the fish all the way in. If we were not wearing gloves the fishing line would have cut up our hands terribly. Sadie and I fought for quite some time but at last a probably four-foot sii fish came up out of the ice hole.

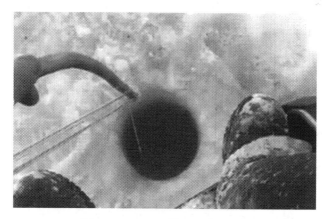

Photo courtesy of Lance Kramer

We love to eat sii fish baked or raw and frozen but dipped in our seal oil. I'm telling you; Inupiat's eat like king and queens. After I caught the sii fish we baked it that evening and it fed all of us. I remember all the adults thanking and praising me for a great meal. I felt so much pride. I had accomplished something that they could not. When the adults were thanking me, I remember even as a little girl how good it felt to catch something on your own. The fact that they were so grateful inspired me too. To this day, I still love to fish. There is something so amazing about fishing to me.

The picture on the cover of this book is our camp Aki, courtesy of Tiffany Scott, Mike's daughter. She sent it to me this last summer not knowing that I was in the process of writing this book. Thank you for the picture, Tiffany, and allowing me to use it. She told me that it was mine to use however I wish.

Aki, is where we spent most of our summers. We have a large log cabin that my grandpa started and worked on until cancer took him. He never got to finish it. After he passed away, my parents and aunts and uncles continued the work until it was complete.

This is where I learned to swim. I got to watch my brother kayak in the lake in front. We used a net to catch hundreds of fish. We cut them and hung them to dry so we could enjoy them with our seal oil for the rest of the year. Seal oil is rendered from seal fat, and we dip everything in the oil. In the same way everyone else uses ketchup, we use seal oil. I cannot describe the taste, other than to say if you get any on your clothing you can never get it out again. It is a strong not fish taste, but an odor that some may find offensive. If you grew up eating it, you cannot live without it. It is amazing and to us it is considered liquid gold. We dip sailor boy crackers, raw and cooked meats and fish, apples, turnips, carrots, pickles, baked potatoes. We even use it as the fat to make Eskimo ice cream. My favorite treat. It has wild Alaskan berries, whale blubber or caribou fat, whipped into an ice cream and it has either salmon, blue or blackberries or any combination of them.

One year my sister Cheree came to visit me in Omaha. She always knew that I missed eating traditional food, so between her and my mom, some of our cousins and Paulette, they always found a way to bring me such great treats. This trip she brought me muktuk, that is whale meat and blubber. Sii fish, dried fish, seal oil and king crab. I cannot tell you how amazing it is to eat such delicacies. She brought a trash bag full of king crab. One of my absolute favorites. Whenever we go somewhere and there is king crab on the menu, I order it. We grew up with king crab right out in the ocean in front of Kotzebue. Even though I cherish every bite of our native foods. King crab is different, probably because it is not as rare of a thing to the rest of the lower 48. Yes, that is what most Alaska Natives call it, the lower 48. I remember sharing just one leg with one of my best friends and she said she sucked every morsel out of that leg and that it was the best she'd ever eaten. Through our marriage I have always told David, "God loves Eskimos so much that He gave us the absolute best diet out there." Ask any Alaska Native, it is the best of any cuisine. Rich in fatty foods to keep us plump for the winter.

Speaking of plump, I never struggled with my weight growing up. When I met David, I was 125 lbs. and wore size five jeans. I wasn't huge into health, but I didn't struggle. After my pregnancies I had a harder time keeping the weight off but also one of the things I struggled with was what I perceived as beautiful. When I was at a women's conference "Women of Faith" I was really struggling with my past. I was praying and crying and really struggling. My husband's aunt Joy was at the conference too and she ran into me. I shared my struggles with her and she just listened and loved me. She was one of the sweetest women I knew next to grandma Breithaupt. That is one of the things we even talked about was how much grandma Breithaupt loved and welcomed us into her and her families' lives. She was the most precious of ladies and I loved her so. I would often tell David she was my grandma and not his. She loved my children like no other and even took them for the weekend multiple times to go shopping and to eat out. Usually junk food. She was just precious to everyone she was ever around but saw her life goal as loving her family and leading and pointing to Jesus the whole way. Whenever I needed my spirits lifted, I drove out to be with grandma and grandpa. I was fortunate enough to live near them in Forks and in Omaha. They were the absolute best examples to me and our children.

At that same conference, I ran into another lady, and I've never told a stranger this before but I said, "You're so beautiful," And she was, I mean stunningly beautiful. Her skin was radiant. She just shone beauty. I said "Sorry, I have never said that to anyone before." She was a stunning African American woman. I shared with her how I was angry at the Lord for taking away my dad and proceeded to tell her how the Lord was present during my dad's passing. She just looked at me and said, "It sounds to me like God was there for you during his passing, and I knew He was, but I was so angry at my dad's dying. We were so close, and his death really hurt me.

She proceeded to tell me how hard she struggled with being beautiful. She said her dad always called her that as he was sexually abusing her and she felt that was her curse. She also shared that someday she wanted to write a book called Beautiful and how the Lord helped her to see she was His beautiful daughter. He was her ultimate daddy. I hope that she did get to write that book. What it reminded me of is my body. Over time, drinking and eating way too much for my comfort was catching up to me and I began gaining weight. At times it caused David and I a lot of anguish but when I realized and never wanted to face was that I chose to keep myself unhealthy because I didn't want to be seen the way I thought of myself. I convinced myself that being heavier and fatter I was safe. I was safe from being desired or even in my own lustfulness being unfaithful. We truly never know the struggles others face.

ARREST

Have you ever been with someone as they are being arrested? Do you know what it is like? I remember one day my oldest son was home from school because he was not feeling well. We were living in a not-so-great neighborhood in Omaha. I looked out my living room window and here is a swat team moving quickly but methodically down the street. It freaked me out and I immediately called David to tell him and he told my son and I to lay down on the floor behind the couch. They had guns drawn and meant business. On one of my mother-in-law's visits, we actually heard gun shots ring out, I never saw my mother-in-law move so fast as she jumped to the ground as shots rang out. Well, this was much different. We later found out that a guy had robbed a bank and ran from the police in our neighborhood.

It brought me back to a time when I was a sophomore in high school. I went to visit a friend, and no one was home. I went to leave and one of my sisters' classmates came running in through the door. It was wintertime and I had just started to get my coat on and head out the door when he ran in and asked If I could give him a ride. Well, we had been busy talking about how no one was home, so I said yes, I'd give him a ride. My snow machine was right out front. When we stepped out the door there were policeman and guns pointed directly at my head. I had no idea what was going on but they handcuffed my sister's classmate and asked me what I was doing at this house. I said that I had just got there when he ran in asking for a ride. They said I should not be with these guys and they were trouble, then said I could go home. I had later learned that he had stolen from a business.

That also reminded me of back when I was going to school in Juneau. David had picked me up from my dorm room, I said that I left my driver's license back in the room and he asked me if I wanted him to go back to pick it up. I didn't want to waste his time, so I told him no never mind. Well, my intuitions are very strong and usually pretty accurate. I try to listen. That evening the police showed up at the apartment we had been renting in downtown Juneau. They had gathered enough evidence to make an arrest, so they were there to pick up David and our roommate. Here we were drinking, smoking marijuana and cigarettes. While they were hand-cuffing David, his roommate handed me the pipe and remaining baggy of marijuana. I quickly took them and put them in my pocket. I looked at him and David like why would you give it to me? His friend said, "Don't worry they won't search you," They didn't but the whole time my heart was racing. I was sure I was going to be caught.

They went through the apartment still trying to gather more evidence of the robberies. They had robbed businesses all along the drive from Juneau to Anchorage along the way. When they were done searching, they took us all down to the police station. David and his friend were in jail the officer asked me for my ID. I said I had left it in the dorms, and I was a college student. I begged for them to just let me go back to the dorm. They said they couldn't until they talked with a parent to see if I was really eighteen years old. They wouldn't take my word for it so they asked me for my parents' phone number and I reluctantly gave it to them. I remember clearly hearing someone else answer the phone. I was sitting across the desk from the arresting officer. And I heard him ask for my mother, "Hello, is this Sophie?" I heard my mom answer, "Yes, it is" and he proceeded to ask if I was over eighteen and that they had just arrested some people I was with.

At that very moment I heard my mom say, "Let me talk to Crystal," I just said, "Mom, it is just a case of being at the wrong place at that wrong time and that I left my ID at the dorm. She was clearly upset but told them yes, I was eighteen and if she's free to go, she may. I had called a friend of mine at the dorm but none of my friends were sober enough to come and pick me up so the officer drove me to pick up items from the apartment and drove me back to campus. All the while I am carrying a pipe and marijuana in my pocket. It was such a scary moment, but I wasn't scared of anything but my mom finding out the truth. I never wanted her to know it was David that was arrested, I just kept saying I was at the wrong place at the wrong time.

My intuitions have served me well. When we were in Omaha, my daughter Hailey and I were walking home after AWANA (a church program for kids where they memorize Bible verses, play games and learn more about Jesus) David was driving kids home, when we got near the associate pastor's house Hailey wanted to run over ring their doorbell and run away. I said why don't you and I just call and say we can see his wife just to scare her. I pulled out my cell phone and the light from the phone scared this man. He was in his car and I had noticed he was just about to get out and I knew by the look in his eyes he meant harm to my daughter. I was thankful that at that moment I just happened to be pulling out my phone. It startled him and he drove away. I grabbed Hailey's hand I did not want to scare her but I said,

"Come on, lets race home." We started to run and at that very moment another car was driving by. I saw the guy turn out of sight and I didn't want him to know which way we went because we still had a couple of blocks to go. It was just starting to get dark so I quickly picked Hailey up and ran for all I could. We got closer to my home, and I saw the man again. At this time an officer was passing by. The man saw the officers and left right away. I ran home with my daughter, thankful that yet again the Lord protected us.

One of our youth group girls began acting up in anger. An anger I knew all too well. I took her out of the youth group and told her we needed to talk. I could tell something was going on and I was concerned for her. I could tell she was not going to say a thing, so I shared a story of one of my cousins, she very reluctantly told me that an adult male was messing with her. It scared her and she wanted it to stop. This too I knew all too well. I am so thankful that her parents were so supportive and were able to put a stop to it. Now she is a beautiful caring mother and I'm thankful she trusted me with her secret.

CAMPING

One year, my sister Cheree and I and some of our friends wanted to go to camp. We begged my dad to take us to Aki. We wanted to go swimming and fishing and just enjoy our camp. Dad finally reluctantly agreed and gassed up the boat and we took off. The cool fresh air was hitting our face and making our hair fly everywhere. I know there can be no way in the world our dad did not have a clue but me and Cheree and our friends were smoking cigarettes out of the canopy on our boat and blowing it and we were convinced that it left the waft behind us, so he was none the wiser. I must believe now that perhaps he didn't want to confront his children. Maybe he wanted to be the cool parent I don't know. But it was so nice and refreshing riding the boat for the couple hour drive. To this day, when I get on a boat I love to ride in the front. Your body crashing up and down and water splashing everywhere as the boat careens through the waves.

My dad was so easy going and just loved to please. When we got to Aki, there were so many mosquitos everywhere. We told dad we wanted to leave. He looked at us like we had just got here, and we did. We parked the boat, jumped out with the anchor and immediately we were surrounded by the pesky little things. We said, "there are too many, we want to go back home," and we did. Just like that. A several hour boat ride just to turn around and go back home. I'm sure it irritated my dad so, but he never complained. He never did. It seemed he wanted only to please his family, all the time. I couldn't imagine all the work that went into that trip just for us to be swarmed by thousands of mosquitos and to tell him never mind, we're done. We didn't do anything else, just complained and grabbed the anchor and headed back home.

One time my sister Cheree and I and one of our cousins were swimming in the river our parents were seining. It is where you pull the net toward the shore and pull the fish in. We were all swimming, and the fish began coming in because they were coming in with the net. It was so cool to have hundreds of fish hitting your body while swimming in the river. I remember grabbing one of them and swimming with it tight against my body. How many people can truly say they went swimming with the fish... ...we could. There are so many amazing stories like that growing up.

One summer my mom, dad, my sister Cheree and I were at camp and the weather got really bad. I cannot remember how long we were there, but I do know we were running out of fuel and food. My mom didn't like to cross the Kotzebue sound if it was at all bad weather or too windy, she usually chose to fly to Noorvik (where my mom was born and raised) and we would pick her up there. If it was windy or bad to cross, she would fly from Noorvik back to Kotzebue and we came in the boat, and she met us with the truck to pull us out of the water.

My dad's maritime call sign was WD40 and everyone in the region knew that name. My sister and I always trusted dad in the boat, and we were always fine. Well, we got to the mouth of Kotzebue sound and the wind and waves were wild. We waited it out for a day or two gathering seagull eggs as our meal, this is a delicacy for us Northwest Alaskan Natives. Eventually, even this got old. That turned out to be the only meal we had for a few days. My dad finally radioed my mom and told her we were going. My mom begged him not to go. But we were out food, time and gas and he said we were going. Well, the weather was really bad. Our boat was going up about sixteen feet in the air and then crashing down, sideways. What is normally about an hour boat ride turned into a five and a half-hour ordeal. My mom, even with the bad weather convinced her close friend's son to take her out in the plane to watch us as we crashed up and down these torrential waves.

I remember my sister Cheree and I sitting on the bench, she had fallen asleep and was leaning on me. I was pushed into the arm of the bench, and it was digging into my ribs and side. It hurt, especially when we crashed up and down. I kept trying to use my floatation device as a pillow for my side because it hurt so bad. We had a blue tarp over our body as the waves were crashing down into our boat. Occasionally my dad would run and grab a bucket and bail out the water that just kept pouring in. In one sense this should have been a scary ride. I knew it was bad out, I know our mother was so worried for us, but I never felt scared. My dad was at the helm, and I knew he would not allow anything bad to happen to us.

When I worked at the Forks Chamber of Commerce in Forks Washington, we got to go on a three-and-half hour whale watching tour. Our captain learned I was from Alaska and without hesitation told me I could navigate the boat. This was so incredible and reminded me of what I was missing in Alaska. I absolutely love to be out on the water, or in an airplane. Riding a snowmachine. Cruising on a four-wheeler, whatever. It brings me such joy. The other boat on our tour ended up having engine trouble so they were towed away. The captain said it was no excuse to end our excursion, so we got to enjoy an even longer tour out on the water. I remember when we were crashing through the waves I sat on the bow of the boat. The wind and waves were crashing onto me, and I was getting wet and cold and I didn't care. It didn't matter... ...I felt like I was home, and I didn't want to leave. The view of the Washington coast and Canada on the other side was so refreshing and brought me back to my childhood. I truly have been blessed to participate in such paradise on earth. Alaska is so beautiful. Words cannot describe it, and Washington to me, has always been a close second.

STUDENT TEACHING

I think every interview I have ever had I share this story. When I was doing my student teaching, I had a student, he was the toughest one out there. Believe me, I've had my fair share. I was a substitute teacher and aide and subbed in all three offices as well in Forks, Washington for over ten years. This student was different. I didn't want him to know where I lived, what car I drove or who my children were. That was the only student I have ever felt this way before. When I started my student teaching process, I remember my cooperating teacher told me he had not had a class like this before ever or since.

The class consisted of about sixteen boys and three girls. I called Daymen Blankenship into my classroom. My cooperating teacher said he needed to see him after school because we both knew he would not receive it well if it came from me. After school Daymen came in and we had a long talk about his behavior and how I saw a leader in him. He laughed and told me I was mistaken, and I told him to watch the class, if he's having a bad day, the whole class is having a bad day. He reluctantly agreed to at least try to listen and behave and see how the class responds. The next day he started the day not listening and then about a quarter of the way through class he hushed the class and said, "Listen to Mrs. Breithaupt." The whole class did.

On my last day of student teaching Daymen jumped up and opened the door for me as I was walking out the door. He became a United States Marine and even came out twice to say hello when my son was first going through boot camp and then at his graduation. My first year of teaching Daymen also came to my classroom and spoke to my students. That is where his wife became interested in him. She was in my first teaching class as well. My fourth period. That class reminded me of Daymen's class. My relationship changed with this young man, and I am very thankful. When I asked him about using his name for this story, he apologized. Daymen, you also changed my life. I'm thankful for every moment I had with every student. I'm proud of the man he became, and I take no credit it is just a piece of my story. Hey, Daymen, I still owe you some gas money.

SPOILED

The first time I tried to ride the bus in Juneau, I had to go to downtown Juneau for something. I am from a small town in Alaska, I did not know the bus system at all. I kept waiting for the bus to get downtown from the UAS campus all day. I did not know that David and my dad were both trying to reach me all day too.

Finally, the bus driver asked me where I was headed, and I told him. He said I was supposed to transfer (get off the bus and onto another one to get to your proper destination). He ended up taking me all the way back to the dorm because it was the end of his route. I called my dad that evening and he called one of his friends to take me to purchase my absolute favorite, my dream car, my red and white 1987 Bronco II. I loved that car so much. So many of my college friends gave me a bad time. They all talked about me being spoiled so I got a vinyl cling for my window that said, "I'm not spoiled! I'm not! I'm not! I'm not!"

During my school years once I started drinking coffee my dad brought me coffee every single morning at my bedside. I still remember talking to college friends about it and them saying, "That's not normal." My only response was, "That's my normal." My dad had such a servant heart. That was one of the reasons I fell in love with David too was his gracious heart. He spoils me all the time too. My dad helped me to know what to look for in a man.

Before I left for college my mom gave me a credit card and told me that it was for emergencies only. As you can imagine a recent high school graduate with a credit card is probably not a good idea. By the time I was on my own, I no longer had that credit card but when my mom came when my son was being born, I asked her if she wanted to go to a local restaurant and told her it was my favorite. She glared at me and said, "I know, I saw it on your credit card bill all the time."

TEACHING

At the time I started teaching alone my first year, after receiving my bachelor's degree, my son Justin was going through the thirteen weeks of grueling transformation as a United States Marine. I wrote him a letter every single day. I'm so proud of my son for serving our country. My niece Dena showed me a picture of Justin and my dad (their Tatta) in their uniforms. Their features are so uncanny. I always thought that my son was a darker, more

Justin and Dad - Marine vs. Army

handsome version of his dad. I was mistaken. He looks just like his Tatta. His Ahna (my mom) and Tatta would have been very proud of him. His Tatta served in the Army. Justin, after five years in the Marine Corps, re-enlisted into the Airforce, because apparently, one branch, one service, was not enough.

While I was teaching, I learned of some temptations my husband was struggling with. The combination of my worry for my son, a debilitating back issue that would later require laparoscopic surgery, and the struggles of teaching my first year (especially my 4th period) proved to be too much for me. My hope and prayer is that Dr. Alford knows her teaching was not in vain. She is a huge inspiration to me and my teaching. My desire is that anyone hurting, in pain or think life is hopeless. It is not. I promise, if anyone draws closer to the Lord, even for one day, by reading my book, then it will have been worth it.

It was not only the pressure of everything that I felt at that time, but it was also the rain in Forks. I hate to say it but rain did not just have an effect on my mother. Every single morning, I woke up, I would hear the rain pouring down like it does in Forks. I felt instant anguish inside of me. It got to the point that every morning I dreaded my alarm clock going off and not just because of my day, but the rain sure brought me down. As soon as I decided to leave, I asked my daughter, the only one living at home, at the time, where she wanted to move. I had been saying Arizona all along and she finally agreed. We left, immediately.

RUNAWAY

Thinking back to my behaviors all the way to me running away from Kotzebue because of what happened to me as a child. I realized that has been my survival mode. When things get tough, I run. I always finish the goals I set for myself, so that has never wavered. I like to check things off my box, which is how I was able to accomplish my hard goals, like getting my degrees, working for certain companies, writing a book etc....

This process has taught me to face my fears. I am doing things I never thought would become my reality. Swimming every weekday, and writing. Cheree has always watched horror films. She still does. As an adult I chose horror movies were not allowed in my house because I realized it was my choice. As I was processing how I chose to run, I thought about the children in Kotzebue and the surrounding villages. They don't get that choice to run. My heart aches for those that are facing their demons every day.

It honestly led me to tears this morning as I was thinking about a child having to wake up and face the person who is doing this to them daily. I was able to run, and it led me to a life of running, but no more. We all get to stand tall and proud because we are loved, and the Lord desires a real friendship with us. We don't have to hide who we are or run. Be who He has created you to be. You will be able to reach someone that I never could.

BLANKET TOSS

Photo courtesy of Jeff Schultz

Sometimes I got to go on the blanket toss up to three times daily. Traditionally, this was used by having the hunter with the best eyesight fly into the air to look for game. What a creative way to find sustenance. The ingenuity just floors me. The blanket is made of a walrus hide that is split in half. Then a rope is woven in and out of the blanket for people to tug. Most people assume that you pull up and down, in this picture you can see all of the tourists that are there, in Kotzebue; but you actually pull towards your body. There were three flights daily full of tourists that flew in from Anchorage. I was the curator at the museum so I got to speak to all of them, three times daily explaining the blanket toss and our cultural dancing. This photo is of me doing the blanket toss outside in Kotzebue. This is what inspired my love for adventure. To this day, my son Justin, is the only one who will go on all of the rides with me at the fair. I loved doing the blanket toss you get thrown so high in the air, especially when there are a lot of people.

DOGS

I absolutely love dogs. They have always been a part of my life and always will be. Anyone and everyone who knows me knows I love dogs, and I always have them. When I couldn't have dogs, I had stuffed dogs, or toy dogs that barked and walked on a rope. To me, they make life better. My daughter has this t-shirt that says, "Be the person your dog thinks you are," and I absolutely love that. They are the best companions ever. Growing up I had a different dog all the time, but they always slept with me or I with them. They are just lovable and just want to please you. Dog people get this, and people who just tolerate dogs don't quite understand it. I've always loved on and talked to and for my dogs. My daughter in law Danie said when she met my son David, it intrigued her that David made voices and spoke for the dog. Then she says and I met all of you and you all do it.

I always wanted my children to grow up with dogs because at times as a child I wasn't allowed to, as much as I wanted them anyway. They just make life so much better that I never wanted to deprive my children of all that a dog brings to your life. I love how they run to you when you have been away. Sometimes you may have been gone for 15 minutes and sometimes an entire day, but they treat you the same when you come through the door. Tails wagging and happy as ever that you're walking through the door regardless of the amount of time you have been gone. They just run to you and play and eat and want to please. That is their whole goal in life is to please their master and spend time with you. They are precious to me and represent what our love should be for our Master (God the Father).

As a child my walls were full of posters of rock bands that I listened to and loved. *AC/DC, Poison, Whitesnake, KISS, Motley Crue*, and more. They covered my entire bedroom. My mom wouldn't let me paint my bedroom walls, so I covered them instead. There was not a single white space on my walls or ceiling. I would get the newest and latest edition of any magazine that had bands I love in them. I was even a member of all of their fan clubs, so I waited to receive items in the mail all the time. Now my walls are full of pictures that I took and hundreds of pictures of my family. My sons and their wives, my daughter and her husband, and my four lovely grandchildren. Everyone always commented on the bedroom with all the posters when I was growing up. Now it is a house of pictures I have taken, places I have been, and family I desperately love. Photography has always been a passion for me since I was in high school in both photography and graphics reproduction (yearbook).

ADDICTION

Addiction is a hard thing. I won't even begin to pretend I understand it. It doesn't matter the addiction. Whether it be food, exercise, sex, alcohol, gambling or drugs. Whatever it is, it is all-consuming. Often your addiction drives loved ones apart. After all, you are choosing that thing over your health or your loved ones. I started smoking marijuana so young, it was hard for me to break. I never understood David's struggle to quit smoking cigarettes, because it was easy for me.

Cigarettes shouldn't bother me. Especially when there are so many other worse things out there. For me, I think it was the secret. He hid it from me and my children for much of our marriage. I believed that if it mattered so much to me, then it should to him as well. For me, it was like infidelity all over again. His cigarettes became the other woman and that is not fair.

OREGON

David and I left great jobs in Arizona to be closer to family and we became homeless. My in-laws fed us because we were out of food and money. We lived in a three-sided barn that was cold and drafty and had Toyota known where we were would have repossessed our car. We ended up voluntarily surrendering both vehicles we were making payments on. This was not at all how we imagined our lives when we got to Oregon. We both thought that we had jobs lined up when we got here and believed we would be living in Salem. Instead, we ended up in Newberg, Oregon.

Even during this, we are ever so thankful and grateful. We survived almost thirty-two hard and trying years together. We have had many obstacles to overcome and by the Grace of God, we have. It took so long for us to find a home to rent in Oregon. Here, your total income must be three times as much as rent. With me not being able to find a job right away, we couldn't find anywhere to live.

Thankfully, we finally found a home. We put an application in for an apartment building and the manager said that they had a waiting list of ten people already. David put his head down just devastated. She finally asked us what we were looking for. David said, "We would love to live in a house. I like to garden and that would be our ultimate choice." She said wait one minute and went in the other room to make a phone call.

When the owners met us, they allowed us to move in to their charming home. It was a three-bedroom, one bath house with a white picket fenced in the front and back yard so we have a place for our dog and for David to garden. Even knowing I did not have a job, and knowing of David's past, they allowed us to move in. They had turned their garage into a living area and completely separated the yards. As always, we have more than we can imagine and better than we deserve! I have had one job after another, and for one reason or another, they ended. We were both happy to be near family, but it has been such a struggle for us financially. We have barely made ends meet, we have not paid a lot of bills and usually would overdraw our account every time we needed to pay rent. It was difficult, but we still believed this was the right move for us as we have been able to do things with our family.

2019

Finally, David got another towing job that came with a beautiful three bed two bath home on thirty-five acres of hazelnuts. We can finally afford to live a decent and good life. The only thing holding me back from telling my story was my work, but I got laid off. If I had not been let go at my new position then I may not have ever picked up my pen again. Yes, I have always been one of those writers. I write everything out in pen. I always have. I cannot complete a coherent thought without first writing it all out. No, I cannot type it, that comes later. It has to be in my handwriting first.

Our children and grandchildren are our greatest pride and joy. David and I could never have asked for better children, and we are blessed to be loved by them. They surprised us with a flight from Portland to LA, and then a four-day cruise to Ensenada, Mexico, for our thirtieth anniversary. I wanted my children to grow up with two parents in a loving home. I never wanted them to have to decide if they were going to Ahna's or Tatta's house.

I know without a doubt we did many things wrong, but I wanted them to know my loving God in the same way and I prayed they each would have a personal and real relationship with God the Father and that He too would become their LOVING

Heavenly Father. I pray the same for my grandchildren that they are raising. That they may know my Lord as their Savior. He is the only thing that is worthy of all our praise. I want my children and my grandchildren to know their hymns like the back of their hands. Know Scripture to help them in their time of need. This is my wish for all. Know Him and know true peace, love and fellowship.

GOD

Just recently I had an aunt say to me, "And he is supposed to be a Christian!" What is that supposed to mean to me? And on the other hand, we hear that a lot as a society. I get tired of the double standard because we do have the Holy Spirit to guide us so we should know better. But on the other hand, we all need Christ, the personal LORD and Savior just as much as the next guy. The reason Christ came to this earth is to save us and we all need it. Some need Him time and time again for the same things. That is the beauty of it, it is a true relationship. He meets you where you are at, when you need it most.

As I go through my journals looking for stories or thoughts that I've missed I have to tell you, the majority of what I read is what the Lord was teaching me through Scripture. I am super far from perfect, not even semi-close but He is not. He loves you wholly and completely; not if and when you deserve it but because He created you and He desires a real relationship with you. You cannot wait until things are right in your life or for another time because none of us are guaranteed time. I promise you, if you seek Him with your whole heart and you desire a real relationship with Him, just ask, He is patiently waiting.

DADS

This whole book, I've addressed women, my daughter, granddaughter, nieces etc.... but I also shared a lot about my dad. When I think about my sons, my grandsons, my many nephews and future great grandchildren I think I have shown you, little girls need their dads. They're going to find men just like they've been shown. Some will be strong and change their ways, but most will find what they've been shown. I wish I learned sooner. Please work hard for what you want. No matter what, there is nothing like the sense of pride for working hard for something. Even as a high school graduate, I was proud because I did it. During my freshman and sophomore year, I didn't care about my grades, then I realized if I wanted to make something of myself, I needed to finish strong, so I did. Please work hard and feel that sense of accomplishment. Then work that hard at your relationships, because they will take work. I know. Thirty-one years is nothing to laugh at. It was never easy, but anything good in life takes hard work and discipline. Work hard, play harder, but love your family first. Your child learns what love is from you. If you want your daughter to grow up and find a fine man than be one so she knows what to look for.

BUSINESS

This year I started my own small business, Ahna's Oils and Salves. I've had a couple people reach out to me like Ahna is spelled Aana in Inupiaq. And while yes this is true, I will never change my business name or the way I spell it because over thirty years ago, I asked my mom how to spell it and she didn't know. I told her over and over again, I need the proper spelling. She assured me she would let me know. It was close to Christmas, and I intended to get her and dad calendars and cups with their only two grandchildren (sons) pictures at the time. It said to Ahna and Tatta, that was the spelling she gave me then, so no, I will never spell it the proper way because my mom thought that was how it was spelled.

A few months into my brand-new adventure, sales were going so well I was so excited. Then suddenly David heard me sobbing from the other room. He came running out and asked me what was wrong. I just held my hand over my mouth and my entire body was shaking. I looked at him not believing it myself, but I said, "I just wanted to call my dad and tell him how my business was doing. It just hit me like a ton of bricks. He has been gone since 2003, almost twenty years ago and I still think I can call him."

Death can be all consuming. And you can have some incredible days and you don't even think about it because it is commonplace. You know in your head that they are gone, and you just go on. And then there are days like this, you wonder how have I gone on this long? I miss my parents. I miss my dad, my biggest cheerleader and my biggest fan!

CHRISTMAS

The first Christmas my father passed away my mom wanted all of her grandchildren home, so she paid my entire family's way to Kotzebue. I was so excited because my children were going to get to experience winter in my hometown. Across the sound behind Kotzebue is what is known as cemetery hill. It is a huge, long hill with one of our local cemeteries on it obviously, but the side that faces Kotzebue is where I spent a lot of time in the winter. It is where a lot of families spend their time as well.

My childhood was spent either climbing the long, straight hill but usually we had a snow machine. My children were completely bundled from head to toe, and we tied the innertube on the back of the snowmachine and headed to the hill. They were shocked by the cold and powdery snow that flew up into their face as the snow machine headed for the hill.

We raced so fast down that hill. There is absolutely nothing that can get in your way when you're zooming fast down this hill. Except for the occasional person climbing up that just happens to be in the way, then it's a quick race to see who gets out of who's way quicker.

I'm sure it helped mom a lot having all her grandchildren at home during that time. We enjoyed a wonderful feast, and she was happily feeding everyone. On Christmas morning she was smiling with joy watching all the grandchildren rip through their packages to find new toys.

NATIVE

I Eskimo danced with the Northern Lights Dancers from fifth grade thru eleventh grade. I love Eskimo dancing. I just smile with happiness. It makes me feel so good inside. It used to be a way to tell stories, but now is for entertainment and joy. At first, I was hesitant about joining because it was so hard to learn. Once I learned though, I couldn't imagine doing anything else.

We traveled all over the State of Alaska for events. I remember dancing in Fairbanks one year and we were so very excited. It had gone so well. We were so proud of our performance. When we walked outside there were green and red lights floating through the sky swishing in and out... we got to see the Northern Lights after dancing. Can you hear me yelling? That is what it was like.

We got the chance to travel to England. The judges at the Nana Museum of the Arctic (where I Eskimo danced for six summers with hundreds of tourists visiting three times a day) were members of the community, who comprised a panel of judges. They were going to watch us and choose ten from about twenty of us to go. I was going. There were others, but I was going.

We had a few weeks before we left for England. My sister Cheree and I were riding on her four-wheeler, and we were hit by one of her classmates right in front of the hotel where probably ten to sixteen people were eating. I didn't feel a thing. No pain. Nothing. I flew through the air. I remember the feeling of not knowing where I was going to land.

Everything was happening in slow motion. It was a cool but beautiful sunshiny day. The first thing I did when I landed was look over at Cheree. She grabbed her injured leg and yelled, "Frank, back up, my leg!" The truck was sitting on top of her leg squished between it and the four-wheeler. As soon as Frank opened up his truck door to get out, I yelled, "Frank! Back up! Her leg!" The very second, I yelled, "Frank" I felt it. The worst pain you could imagine. Something I had never felt before. I reached down with both my hands and grabbed my right leg. Blood stained my new jeans. I saw a huge lump.

I knew right away that Cheree was worse off than I. I just laid there, helpless, watching her scream in pain. Frank's truck wouldn't start. Luckily, there were a fair number of guys eating inside the restaurant. They knew if they just pushed the truck back it could cause more damage. Because it was a Chevy S10, they were able to pick up the front end and move it off of her leg. Cheree started screaming even louder now. I remember my hand clamping shut. The pain seemed to get worse. Someone was holding my leg now.

Cheree and I were taken by medevac to Anchorage, Alaska.

We both suffered compound fractures to our right tibia and fibula. But I was correct, Cheree suffered worse. She had also dislocated her right hip. My sister and I missed over a month of school. We both were in-patients at the Anchorage hospital for two weeks. Then I became an outpatient and Cheree had to stay in traction for another two weeks. We missed dances and it was Cheree's senior year. She loved to play basketball. That was her life. But no longer. She was forced to quit it all. I missed my trip to England.

Not again, a little over a month later there were tryouts for Greenland. This time I was not going to let anything stop me. I had a cast on my leg by this time but there was no way I was going to miss out on another trip. I sat in a tub full of water until my cast softened then I cut if off. The museum director, Phyllis, told us what the judges were looking for. I didn't want the judges to notice that I was in pain, so I forced myself not to limp. I wasn't nervous at all. I just didn't want to fall over in pain. My leg hurt, but I was enjoying myself so much it didn't matter. I hadn't Eskimo danced for two months and missed it immensely.

I thought I did well during the tryouts. The judges left. All of us dancers went into a room. Phyllis walked in and said, "We're tallying up the scores, wait here and we'll tell you who's going." I was getting so anxious. Fifteen minutes passed but it felt like an eternity. Phyllis came in and said "I've got good news and I've got bad news. First, there were a hundred and sixty points possible. We only had one person with a perfect score." She called everybody's name and gave them their score, then looked at me right in the eyes and said, "Crystal got a hundred and sixty points. The next highest was Michael, who got a hundred and forty-six points." I couldn't believe it; I was so extremely happy.

But there was a catch. She said, "Crystal, when we go to Greenland, we're going to be doing a lot of walking, so you can't go." Tears filled my eyes. Everybody was watching me. I tried to suggest many things, but there was no way of changing her mind. I didn't get to go. When I called my mom for a ride, she told me no at first (even in crutches she made my sister and I walk everywhere, how else would we learn) but then I told her my leg really hurt and what I had done. She drove to the museum to pick me up and drove me straight to the hospital where they put my cast back on my leg for an additional three weeks.

PRECIOUS

Cheree and I - Christmas 1980?

The most precious little girl came to the hospital when my sister Cheree and I broke our legs. I always wondered if I would ever be able to find her. When she heard the story of two sisters who broke their leg she told her dad that she had to come to the hospital to bring us two stuffed animals. He took her. The only thing I remember was that she had this long hair and I feel like it was either in a ponytail or pig tails. She brought me this very cute light purple bunny with a yellow sweater. I don't remember what she gave my sister, Cheree. My grandchildren still play with this stuffed animal. I just always remembered her precious heart and that she felt the need to visit the hospital and bring us a toy to sleep with at the hospital in Anchorage so we wouldn't be so scared. What a precious girl, and a great dad to see to it that she did what she felt she should.

CULTURE

Martin Short taught me to Eskimo Dance. There were other teachers but what impressed me was as a young man in his twenties Martin understood that we did not have many elders who knew the songs and the dances anymore. He decided to teach the younger generation so that it would be passed down. There were only about seven elders when I was dancing. Martin had the patience to teach us.

I remember all the girls use to get so upset because traditional dancing women stand still and only bounce their knees up and down. While the men get to hop around, stomping their feet. All of the girls were really jealous of course and during practices we were allowed to jump around as well as long as we were learning the moves, but when we performed, we had to stand with our feet next to each other not moving them. Traditionally women were not allowed to drum either, but he taught anyone who wanted to learn. Our drums are usually made from a caribou hide over a wooden frame that makes a large circle. You drum with a stick that is longer than the circumference of a drum from underneath, hitting the other edge creating the hide to make a sound. Martin taught us younger girls because when the boys danced to a song that was just for them, there were not enough drummers.

When I was learning how to drum, I ripped through the skin of a drum with the drumstick. I felt horrible. Obviously, he was not happy because it is a lot of work to make a new drum. From that point forward we practiced on one made of a tent like material until we knew how. Martin displayed a lot of patience with us but his love for the craft and his desire for us to learn so that it is not a lost art was what really inspired a true love for me, thank you, Martin!

INDEPENDENCE

Traveling all over Alaska with the Northern Lights Dancers gave me a lot of freedom and Alaska Airline mileage. I saw my mom control my siblings with money and I was bound and determined that was not going to be me. So that is why I began working at a young age and have worked all of my life. I do not like anyone telling me what to do. I'm sure you can imagine what a pain that is. David has learned after many years of heartache, I am sure. He will usually suggest 'you should either do this or this.' Praying I choose the one he wishes. Which I usually do because he is much wiser than I am.

Between my junior and senior year of high school I called my cousin George, who lives in Spokane, and I asked him if I could come and visit for a week and if his wife would take me shopping for new clothes. I saved a thousand dollars and he said she would love to so I got my ticket and made an appointment to get my driver's license. Once I did all of that I went to my mom, and I told her what I was doing. She laughed at me and said, "Yeah, right, you're not doing that." I told her I had already got my ticket and spoke with George, yes, I am going. She was so upset with me but she knew there wasn't anything she could do.

I was in elementary school: I remember my dad had these golden walrus head pins. I thought they were my dad's campaign pins, but Mike Scott said that they were available even still today for legislators to purchase and give to constituents or tourists. Well, one of my classmates liked the pin and I told him he could have it for five cents. Then another classmate liked it so I told them fifty cents. I had finally gone up to five dollars apiece and I was selling them too. Me, Cheree and her best friend growing up all began selling them for five dollars.

My mom caught us with the money and told us that it was illegal. With my dad, I knew we were in trouble, but I also can remember that sense of pride on his face. He knew his daughters knew how to hustle.

DRIVING

I failed parallel parking when I took my driving test. I made another appointment for the next day because I was leaving soon. So, I practiced and practiced. I passed. To this day I am still excellent at parallel parking. Well, when I got to Spokane my cousin's wife wanted me to run to her house and grab a pair of scissors because she was cutting someone's hair at their home. I knew I was too stoned to drive, but she assured me I only had to take the first right and I would be on her street. I was not going to tell her I just got my license and I've never driven outside of Alaska. So, I did. I proceeded to miss the turn. I kept driving that same street back and forth until my cousin George finally caught up to me in what seemed like forever.

I kept finding a place to turn around so I would go back and forth on that same street. Mind you, this is before cell phones. I had no directions. And I didn't even know their phone number so I would have had to call my mom. George did find me. And I followed him home. We laughed so hard over the whole situation because when he got home from work the first thing his wife yelled was, "George, I lost your cousin!"

NULLAGMI

My grandma Helen and her mom, my great grandma Jenni would ask me every time I saw them, "Are you still dancing," I would smile big, and say, "Yes," so bold and proud. But you see, Quaker missionaries, who had come to Alaska taught both of them that when we Eskimo danced we were worshiping Satan. Even though as I said before it was the way we tell stories. I told my mom before she died, "You know that is how I became a Christian right mom?" She said, "What?" I said, "Remember they always asked me..." she said she remembered, and she agreed with me. I have no doubt they both prayed for me because they believed what they were told and they did not want to see their granddaughter go to hell.

One of the last things my grandmother said to me when I was leaving for college was "Go and find a good nullagmi boy". That means white in Inupiaq. My husband always says nullagmi is a derogatory statement. I still say no it is not. It means white. My grandma wanted me to find a nice white boy. I still wonder to this day, what she meant by that statement? Did she know I didn't want to find a local boy? Or did she know I was never going to come back? I would love to know exactly what that statement meant. I wish I asked her, but that is what she wished for me. I think she would agree, I did. David is a wonderful father and an amazing husband. He has taught me so much about love and servanthood. I know that everything he does is to make me happier. It doesn't matter if it is a meal, a car, a vacation, or my day. He wants to make it better. He has made me want to be better.

MIKE

Our first family photo - 1994

I don't think that either Mike nor I can explain our relationship. For him, his oldest brother was sent to prison while he was still in high school, and I was just out of high school raising our son David on my own. Our lives changed. Mike has said that my son David is the only baby he has ever held. Our son and the life we knew was forever changed. Mike was also my photographer when David was in prison. He took all my photos of me and my son to send to David. Our first family photo just shakes me. My son was a toddler when my husband got to play his dad. Mike became the coolest uncle to this very lucky little boy.

Mike and I have always been able to quietly talk in the corner of a room amongst the loud Breithaupts. We have always stayed in touch and have seen each other through the worst and the best of things. We have a deep connection with music and with pain. I have been so blessed over these many years of our friendship. I am one of the first to hear his new music.

Mike and baby David - 1993

When I truly believe my book was done, the first words out of my mouth were, "Oh wow, it's done!" This has been not just a grueling process but gut wrenching and writing and rewriting and doubting and questioning, but so healing. I feel like when I wrote my life's work, so did Mike. Two of your songs, *Them Boys* and *Rabbit Hole* have been on repeat for the last two to three years. I know you didn't know what I was up to, but your aches and pains have carried me though. I love you, Mike!

POSSESSIONS

While we were living in Omaha, I learned stuff doesn't matter. I used to care about stuff so much, that people I love were worried about breaking things. I hurt my children over material things. It doesn't matter what the items were. They are inanimate objects that mean nothing in the long run.

Two of my friends took me out to celebrate my birthday. We were out enjoying a nice lunch and David called my friend Diane to tell her not to bring me home and to keep us out a little longer. I knew something was wrong when I saw her reach for our friend Joyce's hand. Together they tried to distract me, but I knew something was up. Diane finally shared that there was a fire in my home today. Now mind you, on Thanksgiving or two prior we went through her sisters' fire where they lost everything. As in, nothing of their home was left standing. All the adults continuously counted six children probably ten times each. They were sitting in the van. We all wanted to be certain the true thing that mattered, their three daughters, and our two boys and a girl were safe and sound.

This one was different. David had been working in the basement where a halogen light stand tipped over. This was my dream home that we and some incredible friends were helping us refurbish. David immediately called the firemen and when we finally got to see the damage, we realized the fire was directly under a gas line where my husband was working. My youngest son was on the second floor playing right next to it as well and my oldest son was on the third floor playing right next to that same gas line. I could have lost all three of my boys in one moment. My youngest was sleeping at a friend's house. Just another time I am aware of the Lord's protection. But I know there are so many more times He protects us, and we carry on totally unaware.

This is how I learned material things do not matter. Your loved ones are what matters. Your children will grow faster than you can imagine, even when you're in the thick of it, and you feel like it will never end. It will end quickly; your children will grow and leave the home and you will question everything you have ever done and often times wish that you understood this when it mattered.

LAUGHTER

My son David knows I am writing this book. He had a clue to what it was, but not everything. I was worried about how he was going to take me writing this book, the most. My son was named after all three of the David's before him. He has a precious heart. I have been trying to reassure him, this has been so healing and it has. We were talking about a book he had recommended to me, *"You Don't Have to Say You Love Me"* by Sherman Alexie. He had just listened to the audio version and wanted me to listen to it as well. I did. For six days I listened to his story. It was so reminiscent of my story I couldn't believe it. I have also been listening to *"Father and Farther"* by Jim Boyd and Sherman Alexie.

My friend Rebecca Mix said that song was my anthem. I think they would disagree, but for me, it was everything I needed to keep going. You see, Rebecca read my words. She edited and scrutinized my writing. That is what she is to me, the person I trust for me to tell my story. She and her husband Ken worked so very hard and for so many years with the Tlingit tribe and they loved them dearly. Ken loved the Inupiaq people and probably knows more of the Inupiat language than I. They were also my bosses at Cape Fox Tours in Ketchikan, Alaska. I was not only blessed enough to share my Inupiat culture with the hundreds of tourists that flew into Kotzebue three times daily. But I also got the privilege of sharing the Tlingit culture in Saxman Native Village. I lived in Ketchikan, and I worked with them and shared their culture. David drove the tour bus and would occasionally bring a group out to see us.

Anyway, my son said that Alexie's story hit a chord with him. It really hit a chord with me as well and gave me the courage to share my story. Well, we got a copy for my husband, and he was having a harder time reading it. He didn't relate to the story. For me, I would occasionally text my son and say, is he writing about me? Or you? Or my mom's story? It was just written in such a way that I related and so did my son. But my husband, it was a hard read and he just didn't get it. I told my son, I'm glad he doesn't relate to it. That is how you children survived. I did try my best, failed a lot, but my husband, he grew up in a Christian home, this didn't relate to him, and again, I am thankful. Because with his upbringing, we could be whole and healed. He was always the sound parent. He had patience to teach my children, far better than I could. My children also got glimpses of what my life could have been. Every time my sister would come with her children to visit, or we went to Kotzebue, they got to see what I could have been.

I have a feeling many will be surprised by this book, Crystal seemed so happy or normal or whatever they'll say. All I can say is the love of the LORD does great things. Also, laughter. I love to laugh. For my senior prom they gave me the "Loudest Laugh Award" when I read it, I laughed so loud and the junior class that awarded me the prize all said, "See!"

Comedian, Don Burnstick, has this amazing set about native women's laughter. And his description of our laughter is so accurate. I often would watch it or recommend others to because it is a beautiful thing. I think it is the Lord's way of protecting and prospering us. We laugh in spite of the pain we've seen or lived.

NOW WHAT?

I realized one of the reasons I always felt like an outsider, and I don't belong was because I did not feel safe. As I said, I run when times get tough, but no longer. I've realized my strength and I knew I had to be strong for my many nieces that I love so dearly and for any girl from a small town like me.

My biggest struggle on my recent trip to Alaska is honor and respect. I believe those are earned titles. My dad, Senator Frank R Ferguson and Doctor Oliver Leavitt, who was like a second dad to me, these men earned our honor and our respect. I am struggling with some leaders I have seen that have been given respect and even honored by our region, and our corporation. They have turned a blind eye to what that responsibility truly means. Why have we allowed rapists to be leaders? Why are we honoring men who have none.

Crystal F Ferguson Qiġñak Breithaupt

MY SCAR

My scar is here today
But it won't be here tomorrow

For I know when Christ comes
He'll take away my tears and sorrow

When we get to heaven some day
He will look at me and say,
I loved you before I created you
And my love for you has never changed

You are my child and have come to
realize
that you need me each and every day
I'm here for you from now
till eternity.

As He opens His arms of Love
In heaven up above
The only scar we'll see
Is the one that shows
He died for you and me

Printed in the United States
by Baker & Taylor Publisher Services